# CUB TO PANDA

## ANIMALS GROWING UP

Jason Cooper

Rourke

**Publishing LLC**
Vero Beach, Florida 32964

www.rourkepublishing.com

PHOTO CREDITS: Cover, Title Page, pp. 4, 17, 18, 21, 22 © Lynn M. Stone; pp. 7, 8, 10, 12, 15 © Keren Su

Title page: *This female will live apart from other adult pandas except during very short periods when she travels with a mate.*

Editor: Frank Sloan

Cover design by Nicola Stratford

**Library of Congress Cataloging-in-Publication Data**

Cooper, Jason, 1942-
  Cub to panda / by Jason Cooper.
      p. cm. — (Animals growing up)
Includes bibliographical references (p.  ).
Contents: Giant pandas — Newborn cubs — Panda cubs growing up.
  ISBN 1-58952-692-9 (hardcover)
  1.  Giant panda—Infancy—Juvenile literature. [1. Giant panda. 2.
Pandas. 3. Animals--Infancy.] I. Title. II. Series: Cooper, Jason,
1942-   Animals growing up.

  QL737.C214C66 2003
  599.789—dc21
                                                           2003007269

Printed in the USA

CG/CG

# Table of Contents

# Giant Pandas

Giant pandas are big, furry **mammals**. They are the most unusual of the world's eight kinds of bears.

Pandas are unusual bears for many reasons. One is that they live almost entirely on bamboo. Another is that pandas have a thumb-like **digit** on their front paws. The "thumb" allows a panda to grasp a bamboo stem as easily as a person grasps a pen or pencil.

*A panda easily holds a bamboo stem and guides it into its mouth.*

# Newborn Cubs

Giant pandas live in cool, moist mountain forests in parts of China. There a mother panda gives birth to a single cub or twins. She rarely has triplets. Cubs are usually born in August or September.

*A mother panda cradles and licks her tiny cub.*

The mother panda usually takes care of only one cub. She almost always ignores any other cubs. Without their mother's warmth and milk, the "extra" cubs soon die. This is nature's way of making sure that the panda will raise at least one cub.

*Helpless at birth, a panda cub's survival depends completely on its mother.*

Unlike some baby mammals such as horses and cattle, a panda cub is helpless at birth. Its eyes are closed, and it has very little fur. It weighs no more than a fat hamburger. It depends totally upon its mother for warmth, protection, and food.

A mother panda snuggles her tiny cub. For many days, the mother doesn't even leave her cub to eat! Meanwhile the cub grows by drinking its mother's milk. Even helpless and blind, a panda cub **instinctively** finds its mother's milk.

*A mother panda gently tends her days-old cub.*

Before a panda cub is a month old, it has the black and white markings of an adult. Soon afterward the cub opens its eyes and begins to crawl. When the mother leaves to eat, she hides her cub from **predators** such as leopards, bears, and **martens**.

As a three-month old, the cub can walk and stand. And by the age of four or five months, the cub begins to roam with its mother.

*A panda cub takes a few steps into a snowy new world.*

# Panda Cubs Growing Up

At four to five months, the cub is about 16 inches (40 centimeters) long and weighs about 13 pounds (6 kilograms). It begins to sample bamboo.

The panda cub found its mother's milk by instinct. But as it ages, it learns some things by traveling with its mother. The cub learns where to drink and where the bamboo grows. It learns to tell one sound from another and how to climb.

*A panda cub learns how to be a panda from its mother.*

A panda cub learns how to be a panda without its father. Adult male pandas live alone except when courting females.

At the age of eight or nine months, young pandas no longer **nurse**. The mother pushes them away if they try. Now their diet is water and mainly the leaves and stems of bamboo. As an adult, the panda will spend nearly 12 hours a day eating bamboo.

*A panda cub looks over its forest home from a tree, where it may take a nap.*

A panda cub remains with its mother until it is at least 18 months old. By the time the cub leaves, it can make its own way in the forest. And by this time, the mother panda is ready to start a new family.

The cub seeks a **home range** of its own. It may travel for awhile with another youngster. But the cub will spend most of its time alone.

*This young panda is old enough to live on its own.*

A panda reaches full size when it is five or six years old. It weighs from 165 to 300 pounds (75 to 136 kilograms). Now it is old enough to seek a mate.

At least one captive panda lived into its 30s. But pandas in the wild don't live nearly that long. Life in the wild has many dangers. Even after pandas have outgrown predators, they must deal with disease, fires, floods, food shortage, hunters, and a loss of **habitat**. There may be as few as 1,000 pandas living in the wild.

*Young pandas traveling together decide to share a tree.*

*Like other bear cubs, pandas are playful as youngsters.*

# Glossary

**digit** (DIJ ut) — the tip of an animal limb, such as a claw or toe; a finger-like extension

**habitat** (HAB uh tat) — a special place where creatures live

**home range** (HOME RAYNJ) — the area in which a particular animal of a group lives

**instinctively** (in STINGK tiv lee) — acting with the behaviors with which an animal is born, rather than acting with learned behaviors

**mammals** (MAM ulz) — a group of milk-producing, warm-blooded animals with fur or hair

**martens** (MART unz) — sleek, tree-climbing weasels of the forest

**nurse** (NURSS) — to give a mother's milk to offspring, or for offspring to take mother's milk

**predators** (PRED uht urz) — animals that hunt other animals for food

# Index

## Further Reading

Leeson, Tom. *Panda*. Blackbirch, 2000
Stone, Lynn M. *Giant Pandas*. Lerner, 2002
Theodorou, Rod. *Giant Panda*. Heinemann Library, 2001

## Websites To Visit

nationalzoo.si.edu/Animals/GiantPandas/
www.sandiegozoo.org/special/pandas/

## About The Author

Jason Cooper has written several children's books about a variety of topics for Rourke Publishing, including the recent series *Eye to Eye With Big Cats* and *Holiday Celebrations*. Cooper travels widely to gather information for his books. Two of his favorite travel destinations are Alaska and the Far East.

ML                                    11/04